Let's Learn About…
Dogs!

Cheryl Shireman

ISBN: 1475291531
ISBN-13: 978-1475291537

DEDICATION

This book is dedicated to Anna Lee - my favorite toddler.

With much love, Bomb Bomb

Some dogs are little.

Some dogs are big.

Baby dogs are called
puppies.

Puppies grow up into adult dogs.

Some dogs are one color.

Some dogs are two colors, or even more!

Most dogs are good at
swimming.

Many dogs are good at jumping.

Some dogs have short hair.

Some dogs have long hair.

Puppies are born in groups
called litters.

Many brothers and sisters can
be born in one litter.

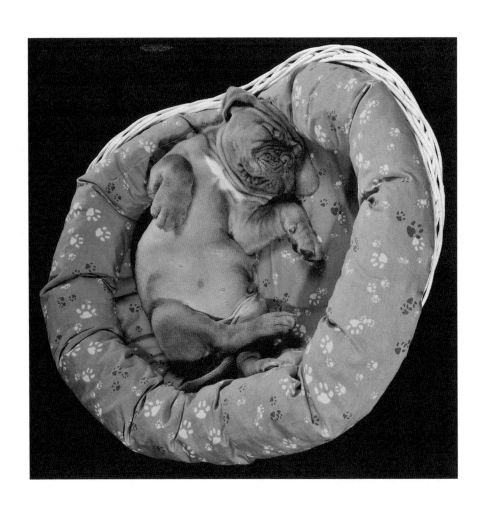

Some dogs like to sleep.

Some dogs like to play!

Dogs depend on us to feed and water them.

We help them to take a bath
too.

Some dogs have long noses.

Some dogs have short noses.

Dog's feet are called paws.
Their fingernails are called
claws.

When a dog walks on soft
ground, he leaves his paw prints
behind.

Some dogs like to explore.

Some dogs like to cuddle
instead.

Dogs like to play with balls.

Sometimes they chew on
shoes!

Some dogs have ears that stand up.

Some dogs have ears that hang down.

A dog will be your friend, loyal
and true.

Be nice to a dog, and he will be nice to you.

 The end.

We hope you enjoyed this
Curious Toddler book.

More fun titles coming soon!

More Books for Kids!

Novels by Cheryl Shireman

ABOUT THE AUTHOR

Cheryl Shireman created the Curious Toddler Series. Cheryl is
married and lives in Indiana on a beautiful lake with her
husband. She has three grown children and one adorable
granddaughter.
Cheryl also writes novels for big people.
All of her books can be found on Amazon and other retailers.
Her website is www.cherylshireman.com
She can also be found on Twitter and Facebook.

Made in the USA
Lexington, KY
06 May 2014